HUMBLE PIE

WRITTEN BY KAREN BACHMAN THULL ~ ILLUSTRATED BY NATALIE FINAZZO

Grow's Grow!
Kate Bachman Thull

General
Higgins ~
Shine On!
Natalie
Finazzo

To our precious family and friends, and to all who shine brightly
in the direction of their dreams

For Matt, Marion, Lynn & Todd, my shining examples of love's pure light. ~karen

To Daniel and Lauria, who believe in me always and
taught me that the stars are within reach. ~natalie

ISBN 978-0-9819860-1-2
Amber Skye Publishing LLC

Library of Congress Control Number: 2009908504

Printed in the United States of America

First Printing: August 2009

13 12 11 10 09   5 4 3 2 1

Edited by Kellie M. Hultgren

To order, visit www.iluminatebooks.com. Reseller terms available.

This story will surprise the kids
who think they know it all,
And those who forget important things,
and want gifts big and small.

This happened to Nellie, a little girl
who said she was the best.

Of all her friends, she thought
she was the cutest and best—dressed.

Nellie stomped her foot and crossed her arms
when things weren't quite her way.

SOLD OUT

Starring Lake Hills
SLED RENTAL

On top of that, she bossed and bragged
and seemed to frown all day.

She had piles and stacks of books and
toys, yet wanted even more.

So Nellie took crayons and paper from
her writing desk's top drawer.

Deciding to write a letter to the big man in the North,

Nellie pondered what she wanted
on the eve of the twenty—fourth.

The list was long and detailed too — just look at what she wrote:

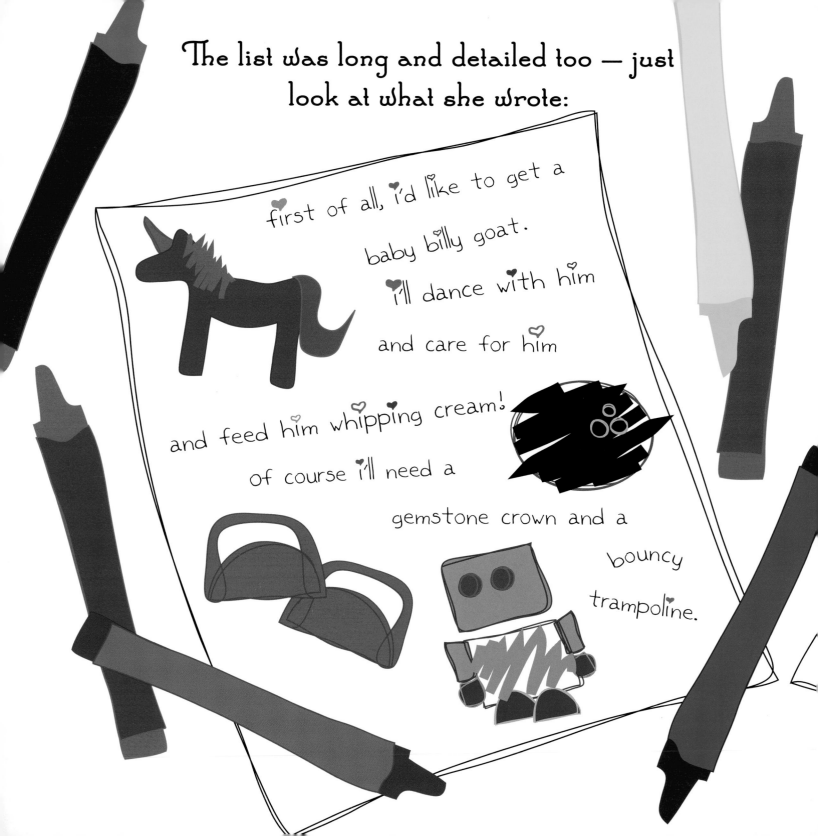

first of all, i'd like to get a baby billy goat. i'll dance with him and care for him and feed him whipping cream! of course i'll need a gemstone crown and a bouncy trampoline.

i also want a bowling ball and shoes
that sparkle red, a robot and a unicorn—
and my ponies need a shed!

a water pistol,
new barettes, and a year's supply of jelly.

that is all for now, i think.

signed,
your
best friend

Nellie

She put the letter in the mail and
went about her days,

Sulking, whining, bragging, boasting
in every single way.

Just before Christmas Eve, Nellie
saw something quite shocking:

Hanging with such tender care
was a surprise within her stocking!

It wasn't a goat or new barrettes — she
looked not once, but twice!
Instead, she found a paper scroll
with a letter of advice.

My Dearest Nellie, greetings!
I have received your list.
I'm sorry to report this year
there's going to be a twist.
You will not get a trampoline
or a year's supply of jelly.
What you will get is Humble Pie,
my darling, dear, sweet Nellie.
Use this recipe for Humble Pie,
it's the perfect way to start,
to find the right ingredients
for a thankful, glowing heart.

Santa

Here are the items you will need to make a Humble Pie:

Simply start with happiness and a twinkle in your eye.

Heaps of care and gratitude are essential to begin,
Then add a dash of honesty and sweetness from within.
You'll benefit from mixing in respect, and be polite.
Stir in some generosity and it will be just right.
A little sprinkle of confidence will add a touch of spice;
Blend that well with giving compliments so very nice.
Put this in a heart that's warm and waiting to receive.
This food for thought will feed all people hungry to believe.

"No presents!"
Nellie gasped, and then she cried out in dismay.

My Dearest Nellie, greetings!
I have received your list.
I'm sorry to report this year
there's going to be a twist.
You will not get a trampoline
or a year's supply of jelly.
What you will get is Humble Pie,
my darling, dear, sweet Nellie.
Use this recipe for Humble Pie,
it's the perfect way to start,
to find the right ingredients
for a thankful, glowing heart.
Santa

"Uh oh! My bossiness and whining
have turned away the sleigh!
Could it be this recipe can help both girls and boys
To glow and grow in love and light and share in others' joys?"

Nellie learned to be content without complaints or grumbles
Revealing not a selfish heart, but one so bright and humble.

Nellie thought about the recipe and knew she had been wrong.

These ingredients weren't hard to find — she had them all along!

Eggs and flour and gratitude went
flying through the air!

She mixed and baked with thankfulness
these Humble Pies to share.

Nellie knew that she might not have boxes with big bows,
But baking up her Humble Pies would
make her Christmas glow.

Nellie beamed with love and light and stirred up brand new starts. Her modesty and care for others fed happy, humble hearts.

So bake your pie with cherries, apples,
or chocolate caramel pieces,

And always know that when you give,
what you get back increases.